The Hearing HEART

by
Dr. Billye Brim

Unless otherwise indicated, all scripture
quotations are taken from the
King James Version (KJV).

Published by
A Glorious Church Fellowship, Inc.
aka *Billye Brim Ministries*
aka *Prayer Mountain in the Ozarks*
P. O. Box 40
Branson, MO 65615
(417) 336-4877

Printed in the United States of America

PREFACE

If you've ever struggled and failed to hear the voice of God, the message you're about to read is bound to excite you. I believe it's a message for this hour. It's the calling of the Lord to the ear of your heart. I received it directly from the Holy Spirit years ago during a camp meeting in Nashville, Tennessee. But before you read about you how it happened, let me explain something.

There's been a pattern of supernatural revelations in my life and they almost always come the same way—through words. I'm not one who receives visions of Jesus but unusual things will happen to words as I am looking at them. They will change right before my eyes. And when they do, the Lord will begin to speak to me. Then the message is confirmed to me in the written Word of God.

That's what happened when this revelation first came to me that day in Nashville. I believe it will bless you as it did me then and every day since.

Billye Brim

The Hearing Heart

As people privileged, even chosen, to live on earth during the last days of this age, it is critical that we hear God's voice and obey Him. Individually, our success and even our very lives can depend upon hearing His instruction in the minute details of life. Nationally, our countries may avert catastrophe and even goat-nation status depending on our receiving and answering Heaven's alerts. Corporately, the Body will be led into Gloriousness by hearing and following its Head.

The Ear of the Heart

"The hearing ear, and the seeing eye, the Lord hath made even both of them" (Proverbs 20:12).

In June 1989, the Lord gave me a supernatural glimpse into the "hearing heart." When it came, I was standing alongside other guest ministers at Pastor Charles Cowan's Campmeeting in Nashville, singing at the top of my voice. I had just taken note of how especially anointed our praise was when something started happening. As I read the lyrics projected onto the screen, one of the words started to change before my very eyes.

It was a word I'd read thousands of times, yet never had I seen what I saw that day in the word "heart." First the **e** popped out...then the **a**...then the **r**.... The **e a r** stood out boldface in the middle of the word like this: h **e a r** t.

As I watched, I heard the voice of the Holy Spirit within me say, "The ear that you hear Me with is in the center of your heart. I put it there. And I amplify it."

I watched the word change as I listened to Him speak: "The ear—h**ear**t—that you—h**ear**t—Me with is in the center of your heart—h**ear**t...I put it there and I amplify it."

Immediately, this impressed my spirit: *The Lord is going to amplify the ear of the heart in the Church, in these last days.*

A Revelation: A Need

Just a few days later, an immediate personal need for such a revelation arose. Still out on the same ministry trip, I was preaching in Kentucky on Sunday morning, June 18, when an emergency call came to rush home. My baby granddaughter was being born prematurely. Grim news met me at the hospital. The doctor said, "She may well be the sickest baby in Tulsa. She probably will not live through the night. If she lives she cannot develop normally. Her brain has been without oxygen too long."

Thank God, within the ear of my heart, I heard words quite different from those of the medical report. My soul and my body were numb. But from the recesses of my spirit, God's promises of life and healing sprang forth.

The Holy Spirit brought to my remembrance the phrase I'd heard a few days earlier, but this time the emphasis was like this: "The ear that *you* hear Me with…."

We had a choice. Her parents and I chose to hear Him. We chose to listen to our hearts where God was speaking. We heard what His written Word says. And we took a stand of faith in agreement with our hearts. Today, Quatsie is beautiful, especially bright, and a blessing to all. Every time we look at her our hearts overflow with thanksgiving to our Lord.

A Revelation of Corporate Glory

A few weeks later, as I meditated on what I had seen in Nashville, this phrase was spoken into my spirit by the Spirit of the Lord: *"The hearing ear in the hearing heart will lead the Church into glory."*

I knew I had another piece of the puzzle! For a revelation of the *Glorious Church* (Ephesians 5:27) had been coming to me little by little for years. One word it started with was, "The Captain of our salvation is leading many sons into glory" (Hebrews 2:10). Now that phrase took on added significance as *He will lead us into glory through the ear of our heart*—the Church will be led into Gloriousness by the voice of God within our spirits.

The Silent Years

I was reminded of Jesus and what Clara Grace was shown about how God the Father taught the Son during His earth walk.

Sister Grace, a respected minister of the Gospel, was a prophetess. The first time I heard her was April 24, 1967 at Brother Kenneth E. Hagin's seminar just two days after I'd received the baptism with the Holy Spirit. She was about 75, and the first woman preacher I'd ever heard. My denomination purported that women could not preach. Yet I sensed God's presence as she spoke. Sister Grace was a mentor of Jeanne Wilkerson. Sister Wilkerson told me that Clara Grace had more experience, "beyond the veil" than anyone she knew.

In 1969, Sister Grace sat down with two young ministers and shared with them some of those experiences. Many years later, a cassette tape of the "precious things" she told them came into my hands.

Clara Grace said of her visions; "The Lord takes me into the realm of the Spirit… when that happens, I don't know one thing that's around me, but I'm very conscious of my own entity and of what I'm seeing, and what I'm hearing."

In the vision that came to my remembrance, Sister Grace was in the carpenter shop watching Jesus complete the last table He made before entering His ministry. He took no short cuts. She saw Him finish and polish the table well. He cleaned His tools and put them neatly away. Then He turned to her and stretched out His arms. She knew to step into Him, put her arms where His arms were, and her legs where His legs were. She said, "At once I was as big as the universe and as small as the tiniest particle in it."

Knowledge came to her where the Bible is seemingly silent—the eighteen years between Jesus going up to Jerusalem at age 12, and the start of His ministry at age 30. It was revealed to her how God the Father taught His Son. She saw that Jesus had to have revelation of the Word of God and His place in it—*for the One who had walked up and down through eternity had laid aside His glory and became as we are.*

I have since misplaced the cassette of Sister Grace's vision, and I don't remember just how these Scriptures came. But the following two passages especially demonstrate the Father's teaching and the Son's learning. The emphasis and comments in brackets are mine.

> Psalm 119: 97-102
> 97 Oh how I love thy law! It is my meditation all the day.
> 98 Thou through thy commandments hast made me wiser than mine enemies [God taught Him; God made Him wiser]: for they are ever with me.
> 99 I have more understanding than all my teachers: for thy testimonies are my meditation. [Notice the place of meditation of God's Word.]
> 100 I understand more than the ancients, because I keep thy precepts. [Verses 99 and 100 calls to mind His sitting in the midst of the doctors at 12, astonishing them with His understanding and answers.]
> 101 **I have refrained my feet from every evil way, that I might keep thy word.** [Only the Messiah, not David, kept His feet from every evil way.]

102 I have not departed from thy judgments: **for thou hast taught me.**

This next passage in Isaiah 50 reveals that the Father opened His Son's "ear to hear" and how the Son "kept His ear open" to the Father.

> Isaiah 50: 4-5
> 4 The Lord God hath given me the tongue of the learned [the taught], that I should know how to speak a word in season to him that is weary: he wakeneth morning by morning, he wakeneth mine ear to hear as the learned [taught].
> 5 The Lord God hath opened [Hebrew *pathach*: opened wide, plowed, carved out] mine ear, and I was not rebellious, neither turned away back.

In the vision, Jesus told Clara Grace, "I never laid down My head to rest without meditating the Scriptures and Who I was in them."

This we see in Psalm 119 and Isaiah 50, as quoted here. He meditated the Word and who He was in it, and *morning-by-morning* the Father awakened Him, opening wide His ear to be taught.

Imagine every morning, the Voice of the Father awakening His Son, teaching Him of the Father's plan and His place in it. The Son kept His ear "open" through obedience: "I was not rebellious neither turned away back" (v. 5). He accepted Who He was, and what was required of Him.

> Isaiah 50: 6-7
> **6 I gave my back to the smiters, and my cheeks to them that plucked off the hair: I hid not my face from shame and spitting.**
> 7 For the Lord God will help me; therefore shall I not be confounded: therefore have **I set my face like a flint,** and I know that I shall not be ashamed.

My heart is deeply moved when I consider it. Yet surely one can scarcely imagine how it must have been when Jesus first saw (during His earth walk) that these Scriptures prophesied of Him. That He was the One of whom they spoke. That He must give his back to the smiters, His cheeks to them that plucked off His beard, and His face to shame and spitting. Yet God would help Him. Therefore, He set His face like a flint knowing He would not be ashamed.

Who We Are In Him

Through the 1970s, I was editor-of-publications for Kenneth E. Hagin. When people asked him to recommend a way to study the Bible, he usually told them what he considered the most important Bible study Christians could make. He advised them to look up in the New Testament Epistles phrases such as "in Him," "in Christ," "through Christ," "in the Beloved," etc. In other words, Scriptures which tell Christians who they are, or what they have, because they are "in Him."

He advised people to underline them, write them down, and meditate on them. And he advised that they make them their own personal confessions.

Brother Hagin often taught on this subject, and in the mid-'70's we put those teachings into a mini-book entitled *In*

Him. At the end of that book we listed such verses.

What would happen if we would followed our Lord's example: meditate on the Scriptures, and who we are in them? What mighty growth would take place in the Body of Christ if we individual members (on a wide scale) would meditate the Scriptures before we lay our heads down to sleep, and ponder who we are in them? I believe it would follow that morning by morning the Father would awaken us. Morning by morning the first Voice we would hear would be His, impregnating us with His plan for our day, and for our place in the big picture for these last days. If we accepted and meditated these truths as our own, we would be the "Glorious Church" as revealed in the Scriptures.

Ruling and Reigning

Consider the power and place in God's plan at the culmination of this age, if one adopted this as a personal confession: *He hath quickened me together with Christ...and hath raised me up together, and made me sit together in the heavenlies in Christ Jesus* (Ephesians 2:5-6).

How much more faith would we have that God would use our prayers and declarations in these trying times if we meditated and received as our own: "...much more they which receive abundance of grace and of the gift of righteousness shall reign in life by one, Jesus Christ" (Romans 5:17).

Rather than being afraid at every terrorist threat, we can know that we are "seated with Him at the right hand of the Father," the seat of power. We can like the Master, say what He wants said, and do what He wants done.

Jesus said, "The Son can do nothing of himself, but what he seeth the Father do...I can of mine own self do nothing: as I hear, I judge: and my judgment is just; because I seek not mine own will, but the will of the Father which hath sent me" (John 5:19,30).

I have long believed that we will only do "greater works" (John 14:12) when we can operate as our Lord operated, in such close communion with the Father that we can see and hear what His will is. And I believe this is available to us as it was available to our Lord—if we will do what He did. We can be taught as our Father taught the Master—if we will follow His example. We can have our ears opened wide, dug out, to know the will of the Lord, and then obey Him.

Today If You Will Hear His Voice, Harden Not Your Heart

Soon after the revelation at Nashville, the Lord supernaturally took me through the Book of Hebrews. As fast as I could turn the pages He showed me that the Book was about God speaking to us and our hearing Him, and doing His bidding. As the pages flew by, phrases stood out to me. I cannot fully communicate to you here all I saw and heard, but this is just an example of how it went, and the emphasis given to His speaking and our hearing: "God…who **spoke**… by the prophets…. Hath **spoken** unto us in these last days by His Son…. Therefore we ought to give the more earnest heed to the things which we have **heard**…. Today if you will **hear** His voice, harden not your hearts.... Ye are come unto Mount Zion, and unto the city of the Living God, the heavenly Jerusalem.... To God the Judge of all.... And to Jesus the mediator of the new covenant.... See that ye refuse not Him that **speaketh**...." (Hebrews 1:1-2; 2:1; 3:15; 12:22-25).

In the book of Hebrews, it reveals what Jesus quoted from Psalms, "Wherefore when he cometh into the world, he saith, Sacrifice and offering thou wouldest not, but a body hast thou prepared me.... Then said I, Lo, I come (in the volume of the book it is written of me) to do thy will, O God" (Hebrews 10:5,7).

I decided to look up what He quoted from Psalm 40. Here it was again—how the Father taught the Son.

> Psalm 40:6-8
> 6 Sacrifice and offering thou didst not desire; mine ears hast thou opened [Hebrew: *karah*—digged]: burnt offering and sin offering hast thou not required.
> 7 Then said I, Lo, I come: in the volume of the book it is written of me,

8 I delight to do thy will, O my God: yea, thy law is within my heart.

Like Him, in the volume of the Book it is written of us. All the Bible is for the Church—but not all the Bible is about the Church. Some of the Bible is about other peoples (*The Jews, the Nations, and the Church* [1 Corinthians 10:32]). The part of the Bible that is particularly about the Church is the New Testament Letters. In those Epistles it is written who we are, what we are, and where we are going. I know that the Church would take giant steps toward Gloriousness, if we could do what Jesus did:

1. Meditate on those Scriptures about the Church.
2. Ask the Father to dig out our ears.
3. Do what it takes, to get Him to dig out our ears.
4. Accept and not turn back from His plan for our personal lives, and our part in the Glorious Church He is preparing.

How You Can Be Led By The Spirit

One day in the late 1970s when I was still editor-of-publications at *Kenneth Hagin Ministies,* Kenneth E. Hagin walked into my office and began talking to me. And I used the words as the preface to the book, *How You Can Be Led By The Spirit Of God by Kenneth E. Hagin.* He said, "God has been talking to me recently about something I failed to do. Twenty years ago, in February 1959, in El Paso, Texas, the Lord appeared to me in a vision. He came into my room…sat down in a chair by my bedside, and talked with me for an hour and a half…. He said, 'I did not put prophets in the Church to guide the New Testament church. My Word says, *As many as are led by the Spirit of God, they are the sons of God.* Now if you will listen to me, I am going to teach you how to follow my Spirit. Then, I want you to teach my people how to be led of the Spirit.'"

Brother Hagin felt he had not taught this as he should have. He told me he was going to teach it in an upcoming seminar and one purpose would be to put it into a book. I asked Berta Bass to get me the manuscripts of every time he had taught the subject. One morning I walked into my office and piled-high manuscripts covered the top of my desk. It was my blessed task to go through them and make them into the book.

In the process, I learned what Jesus taught Brother Hagin, "The spirit of man is the candle of the Lord, searching all the inward parts of the belly" (Proverbs 20:27). And I learned how to know the voice of the human spirit, the inward witness, the inward voice, and the Voice of the Holy Spirit. And how to train the human spirit.

Knowing how to hear and follow the Lord has been the key to any success I may have had in ministry. I heard the Lord tell me, "It is time to resign from *Kenneth Hagin Ministries.* I want you to get out of the golden boat with fur lining and walk on the water with Me."

I heard Him tell me, just after Kent (my husband) moved to Heaven in 1986: "Go to Israel and study Hebrew in the Land. I am going to place you close to the Jews."

In 1995, I had a vision. The Lord showed me a bed in a log cabin, and told me to help the pray-ers by going to Branson, Missouri. He told me to build a place dedicated in individual and corporate prayer: "To pray in the plans of God and to stop the strategies of the enemy."

Then in January 1999, I heard the Lord say; "Something is going to happen in Israel in September. And I want you there." That September, He made it possible for us to purchase a place in Migdal *(Magdala)* in the Galilee for His purposes.

Proverbs 20

Proverbs 20 has wonderful verses particular to our subject. One especially pertinent for this hour is in Proverbs 20:5, "Counsel in the heart of man is like deep water; but a man of understanding will draw it out."

He is speaking.

We must listen.

And we must obey!

Tongues and Interpretation through Chip Brim (Tongues) & Dr. Billye Brim (Interpretation) at *Champions 4 Christ* Youth Rally July 31, 2013

Think not that this is a strange thing, but this is a thing of great import. Heaven's court is in session. A gavel is about to fall and the time of the end is about to begin. And so I make a call for those who sit in the darkness and need to see the light.

Some of the darkness is in the dark countries of the earth. China has been mentioned, and other dark places are in what is mentioned also today, from this platform and bars and saloons. Clubs and places, rooms, homes, families that are dark. I will breathe the spirit into those places. I will send the light into those places, now as never before. And I will send it through you.

I have called these who stand before you and many more. They are the laborers of the words which speak of the last hour laborers. And did I not say in My Word that though they go forth in the last hour, they will share a reward as if they had been in the field many years?

You speak of signs, wonders and miracles. They are listed in the books of acts that men have walked in since Jesus came. That Paul did not see, and Peter did not see, and none of those prophets in the New Testament have seen what your eyes will see. For the greater glory and the greater miracles are reserved for the last hour. And the Glory of the Lord will fill you, and the Glory of the Lord will rest upon you, and the Glory of the Lord will minister through your tongues and through your fingers and your very beings. And men shall see, at the very last hour and the very last opportunity, they shall see Me function in the earth through you.

So through the wonders of this hour and the technology as you're watching all around the world, know that these here are symbolic of those I have called in your own countries and to your own places and around the world. I am calling many, many, many, many, many, many, many, many,

many just like this. Making My call plain to them as I did to Samuel. And they have said yes. And they will go in the Glory of the Lord, to the Glory of the Lord. And it shall be thus and so and the time is short. So give Me your ear, give Me your time, I will work with you, you are Mine.

About the Author

Billye Brim's Christian heritage is rich. She sensed the call of God in early childhood. However, it was only after an encounter with the Holy Spirit in 1967, that she as a young wife and mother of four began to follow Him to walk out her call. For almost ten years she served as Editor of Publications for Kenneth E. Hagin Ministries where she also taught at Rhema Bible Training Center.

Immediately after ordination in 1980 she traveled to Soviet Russia in what proved to be ongoing ministry there. Since then she has literally ministered around the world several times over.

Kent and Billye Brim with Lee and Jan Morgans founded a local church in Collinsville, Oklahoma. *A Glorious Church Fellowship* is the foundation of *Billye Brim Ministries* and *Prayer Mountain in the Ozarks* in Branson, Missouri, and the soon-to-be-built *Migdal Arbel Prayer and Study Center* in Israel.

When Kent passed away in 1986, Billye was led to "study Hebrew in the Land." Studying at Ulpan Akiva in Israel led to the unique seminar tours she has guided in the Land from 1986 to now. It also provided a pattern for the prayer and study center in Israel.

"Helping Pray-ers" is a God-given directive in her life. One place this happens is at *Prayer Mountain in the Ozarks* near Branson, Missouri. On 200 plus acres log cabins provide places for individual prayer, or small prayer groups. Corporate prayer meetings are held twice a week in the chapel.

On Wednesdays at 12 Noon Central Time, the meeting is streamed live. Pray-ers (who have named themselves World-Wide Pray-ers) join in united prayer via thousands of computers in more than 60 nations. This prayer is focused primarily on an Awakening to God. For in a corporate prayer meeting in June 2008, Billye Brim and the pray-ers were impressed with these words: *One thing will save America...an Awakening to God. One thing will avail for Israel and the nations, An Awakening to God.* Several thousand pray-ers from around the world gather in Branson for an Autumn Assembly of Prayer she hosts.

Billye Brim is blessed to work with others across the Body of Christ. She strongly believes in walking out what Scripture teaches that we are one Body, with one Head, one Spirit, one Lord....

First Corinthians 10:32 is foundational in Billye Brim's ministry. The "good works that He has ordained that she should walk in" involve activity among the Jews, the Nations, and the Church—all to the Glory of God.

For more information about Dr. Billye Brim:

BILLYE BRIM MINISTRIES
PRAYER MOUNTAIN IN THE OZARKS
PO BOX 40
BRANSON, MO 65615
(417) 336-4877
BILLYEBRIM.ORG